MW01233781

HELLO GOD, IT'S ME AGAIN

HELLO GOD, IT'S ME AGAIN

Jean Edwards

Library of Congress Control Number:		2009911914
ISBN:	Hardcover	978-1-4415-9929-2
	Softcover	978-1-4415-9928-5
	eBook	978-1-4415-9930-8

Photography and artwork by Jean Edwards

Print information available on the last page.

Rev. date: 04/01/2022

To order additional copies of this book, contact:
Xlibris
844-714-8691
www.Xlibris.com
Orders@Xlibris.com
582428

CONTENTS

Hello God, It's Me Again

Hello God, It's Me Again

The great thing about my relationship with you is the accessibility. You're always home and the line is never busy. I have friends I could confide in and ask for help, and I sometimes do, but they are often on the phone, shopping, working or on vacation. I can always count on you. Not by phone or E-mail or even by Fed-Ex. You are there on call whenever I am in need, or desperate, or even when things are going great, and I know I am never alone.

Sometimes I'm a little awestruck by the beauty of the earth, especially at night. I love your night skies and the friendly stars you placed in the heavens, reminding me that you are close by. Thanks, God.

Winter Fog

Winter fog is a strange phenomenon. One usually thinks of fog rising from a river or lake as the sun pulls the vapor from the icy water. Then there is the fog that creeps in from the ocean at any time of year and it is expected to arrive at will. Winter fog is different. It arises in the gloom of day or dark of night, hovering over the snow covered hills and fields. Softly it floats above the ground, as though deciding whether to go or stay, quietly hiding the bumps and stumps, presenting a mysterious tranquility over the land.

Please, God, let me be like winter fog, softening life for others by covering their lumps and bumps, difficulties and heartbreaks with love and understanding.

Hungry Again

I was in town last Wednesday, having multiple errands to accomplish in multiple parts of town. By one o'clock I was ravenous. What better place to satisfy urgent hunger than the fast food burger palace. The line seemed longer than usual and I still had more errands to do. I needed to pick up a suit at the dry cleaners along with two winter coats I would need before the snow flies, and I was really hungry from smelling all the fries and burgers on the grill. Orders were being taken and paid for but it seemed no one was receiving a meal. Oh, now one, but where were the rest? And mine? I was becoming a little antsy so I walked over to the condiment bar at the side and picked up a couple of napkins, a straw and two ketchup packs, then went back to the rail to wait. Poor service, I thought. But then I watched the workers steadily putting orders together. Some were teenagers. Were they saving for college? Some tired looking girls looked to be in their twenties. Were they single mothers trying to make ends meet? Did they have laundry and housecleaning to do, and meals to prepare when they got home? And the older workers in their so-called "Golden Years," were probably earning their prescription money for elder ailment medicine.

I wasn't impatient any more. My troubles seemed so small compared with what those workers might be facing. God, help them. They work for low pay just to make their way in life. Let me never show impatience to those who serve, and remind me to smile and say thank you . . . and maybe a "God Bless You" wouldn't hurt.

Help!

Driving the country roads of Maine in my S-10 pick-up truck is quite pleasurable. The views of trees, ponds and hills ever change as I cautiously watch for deer that might suddenly cross the road, keeping my speed under control. Is that your plan? Sometimes I feel so happy I almost laugh out loud.

I took my sister with me one day and guess what! I had failed to watch the gas gauge. As I was driving up a hill and around a curve, (oblivious to our impending plight) the truck spluttered to a stop. There was no house in sight. I was contemplating the situation when a well-worn auto pulled up behind us. The driver left his vehicle and came to the side of my Chevy and asked if we needed help. Upon my explanation he offered to drive me to town for fuel. Leaving my sister with the truck seemed the wisest course of action. She could lock herself in if she felt unsafe, while I would be brave and get into the car with the stranger, hoping I would not be robbed, strangled, dismembered or worse, and be able to return so we could resume our journey.

The gentleman did indeed take me for gasoline and then safely back to where my sister waited. I never saw that worn car or the scruffy looking gentleman again. Was he one of your angels?

Hello God,

The river is rushing faster than usual since we had a few days of rain. The water jumps and froths with wild impatience in its journey to the sea. But, yet, there are eddies and pools near the edge by the riverbank. It seems to be a mirror of life. There is often too much thrashing towards a destination and not enough calm reflection.

Please help me spend more time contemplating the eddies and pools of life.

Pie

Having company is always fun. With friends coming to visit it seemed like a good idea to bake a pie. It's not difficult as long as there are store-bought crusts and packs of blueberries in the freezer. Letting them thaw an hour was easy, then one doughy crust in the bottom of the pie pan, adding the berries, sugar, and a little flour and cinnamon. Putting the top crust in place went smoothly, pinching the edges to keep the juice from spilling out during baking, marking the top with a "B" with punctures from a fork. Popping it in the oven gave me a "life is good" feeling.

When the crust turned golden I found my potholders, lifted it from the oven and "Oops!" I slipped on a wet spot on the kitchen floor and the pie went flying. What a mess. Quickly rolling up the stained kitchen rug I rushed it to the washing machine and then cleaned the floor, the cupboards, the baseboards. Feeling stricken, I asked you what to do, and it popped into my head that I had a chocolate cheesecake in the freezer. My guests loved it. Thanks for showing me that almost anything can be fixed, but sometimes it has to be replaced.

Rocks

Rocks are fascinating. Sometimes if you roll one over interesting little creatures are exposed. They would have preferred to be left alone there in the darkness, like some people. They would rather be left in the darkness than have their lives scrutinized. Perhaps we wouldn't want to know the things that the light would reveal.

Some people throw rocks. They use words as rocks. They are the worst kind of rocks of all. They hit harder and hurt more. I've been hit by a few. Sometimes I expected it and sometimes it was a complete surprise, from someone I never thought would have a reason to throw a rock at me.

There are some smooth rocks, with no bumps or ridges. When someone throws a smooth round rock it's one that doesn't look like it would give pain at first. As when someone gives a nice-nasty compliment, i.e., "What a lovely new outfit you're wearing, you don't look nearly as heavy in that style," or, "Your hair looks great. I admire anyone that doesn't give in and try to look younger. There's nothing wrong with looking your age," and, "Don't pay any attention to anyone that stares at your feet. If they had your foot pain they would be wearing clunky orthopedic shoes too."

Please, God, keep me from throwing any kind of rocks.

Flowers

Dear God,

Please help me make a beautiful flower garden. I don't have a green thumb but with your help a thing of beauty could be created for everyone passing by to enjoy. It is your sunshine, your rain, your soil, your seeds and bulbs. I have to contribute so little, and on my knees before you is where I should be.

More Trouble

Hello God,

Today I'm dealing with a lot of problems. I'm having trouble wondering why a child is crippled. I need help working it out in my mind. Then there is the problem of carelessness. I hurt someone's feelings because I spoke without thinking, and I need help finding words of comfort and encouragement for a friend battling a serious illness. Illness is hard for me to accept, so please give me insight into your will, and put words of love and courage in my heart that I can share.

Observations

Trees are interesting. Some grow tall and straight; some grow at crooked angles. Many bear good fruit while others bear poisonous (to humans) seeds. Trees seem to start on equal ground but then go their different ways. They are a lot like people.

And then there are roads. They aren't much good if they don't have a good foundation. They break up and have potholes and wash out in wet weather. Oh, they can be patched but they just break up again. They do much better if they are built right in the beginning. Good roads make life easier. One just needs to be sure they take the right one. Is this what you meant by the straight and narrow path?

Hello God,

I got a lot accomplished today. The dishes washed, the house vacuumed, a couple loads of washing done, washed the kitchen floor, mended the pockets of my husband's jeans, ironed a few clothes, called a friend recuperating from surgery, made a salad for supper, whipped some cream to go with shortcake. I'm glad I talked to you this morning before I started my day. Thanks for the help.

Route 66

When my husband and I were young traveling across country to where he was stationed in California, route 66 was the highway to take across the southwest states. It was long and it was straight, with only occasional hills—and it was dark at night. Our little 49 Pontiac scooted along without streetlights or towns for miles on end, with only the white line to guide us. The roadsides were black and mysterious, our headlights the beacons we followed. Occasionally a flash of heat lightening would suddenly light our world, bathing it in a white glare that seemed to last minutes, making the returning darkness even more foreboding following the flash.

We soon found ourselves following an eighteen-wheeler. Mile after mile we followed, then we dropped back as a hill emerged before us. When we reached the crest no eighteen-wheeler was in sight. We hadn't passed a town or even a side road, but the truck had disappeared. We hoped he hadn't gone off the road and crashed. We saw no evidence of that, but we have always wondered. I hope you took care of that driver, God.

Chocolate

I love chocolate. You might say I am obsessed with it. I think I could live on it. I know it's not good for me (at least as much as I would consume if I had the chance) for many reasons—the caffeine, the sugar, the oils, the calories. I could pretend I eat the dark chocolate to "protect my heart." I could pretend to eat it because it keeps me alert when I am tired. I could pretend I buy it to "share," but in reality I just plain love chocolate. I have a friend who gave me a refrigerator magnet that proclaims "Hand over the chocolate and nobody gets hurt." My love of chocolate is legend.

There are ways I control my choco-urge somewhat. There's the money thing, the guilt thing and the "I'll get caught hogging it" thing.

Please, God. Help me remember there are children in the world who don't even know that chocolate exists. Help me by laying it on my heart to give to the hungry instead of myself.

Wrinkles

I've been concerned lately about the way my face looks. I've never been a great beauty but as the years go by I've acquired a wrinkle here and a sag there. Someone asked me how I received the scar in my eyebrow and I had to admit it was a wrinkle and not from some great adventure, like being gored by a bull while on safari in Africa. I don't mind the ever-whitening hair. Platinum blond is not the sole property of the elderly, and besides, it goes well with the pale complexion I have acquired from avoiding the sun in an attempt to prevent brown spots from sprouting.

The thin skin on my hands with the map of New York City traced in blue veins doesn't bother me much. Red nail polish pulls the eye away from the aged look and makes it all quite patriotic. My hands don't hurt and they work well so I have no complaints. Which brings me back to the wrinkles. Saying "I earned them," or "I'm proud of my laugh lines," doesn't seem to work. I guess you want me to do the best I can with make-up, and forget about what I can't change and just accept them as part of your plan.

Please, God, help me accept life as it is.

Frustration

I understand frustration. Making Holiday cookies seemed like a good idea. Someone told me it would be easy if I mixed up a big batch of basic cookie dough, baked a pan of the cookies, then added nuts to the remaining dough, baked another pan, added M&M's, baked another small batch, repeated the former by adding cocoanut, and baked them.

The first batch seemed to spread out too much and sort of melted together, making them look ragged when I cut them apart with a spatula. (Didn't taste bad, though). I added some flour along with the nuts on the second batch, dropped them by teaspoonfuls on a baking pan. They came out O.K. Next came the M&M batch. 'Didn't have enough grease on the baking sheet so they stuck on and it was a mess. I had a mound of sticky crumbs. 'On to the cocoanut batch! I had accidentally hit the temperature control knob and burned those up. From my batch of dough I got one dozen good cookies. Is this your way of telling me short cuts aren't always a good idea?

Hello God,

I've always wished I had musical talent. I watch others play the piano, strum a guitar and sing. How I wish I could sing. It's not just that I have a squeaky, gritty voice. I can't carry a tune. I love being in a crowd or choir where I can pretend I am singing. I sing (if you can call it that) very softly and make believe I am a part of it. I revel being in the midst of all that beautiful sound. And harmony. It's most amazing. I marvel that some can sing notes just off the tune and make such melodious music. When I sing a little off the melody it is ear torture.

Do you think someday you could find a place for me in one of your choirs when I get my new voice?

Winterberries

What an interesting bush is the shrub of the genus "Ilex," otherwise known as the "winterberry." The bush itself is quite unobtrusive. One hardly notices it through spring and summer, but when winter comes "viola." The cheerful bursts of color liven the winter landscape as well as the hearts of all who are fortunate enough to enjoy their cheer.

Strangely, they get their color as the last autumn leaf drops, bursting forth just as all the hues of summer have faded. They arrive as a saving grace, lest winter be too drab and depressing. They remain untouched by birds or fauna due to being blessed with an unpleasant flavor, and are not eaten until all other seeds and berries are consumed. We are encouraged by their presence until it is time to anticipate the first crocus. What a great plan you designed!

Gluttony

They say I was born skinny. Pictures show that I was thin for quite a few years. Of course being picky about food helped keep me that way. Everyone urged me to eat more and get some "meat on my bones." I was persuaded to try more and different foods and "develop" a taste for them. Boiled fish still gives me a weird case of the shudders but I learned to like gravy (as long as it's not the white kind) onions, (chopped, raw or fried) sour cream on baked potatoes, stuffing with turkey and coffee with only cream. Nothing convinced me to eat okra, which has always looked and tasted like a freak of nature to me. I have an aversion to eating things with hair. Ice cream was A.O.K. with me from the day I was born on that cold winter's morn, as far as I know.

Since I have "matured" both in food taste and personal size, I face the problem of "food control." Almost everything tastes great (except of course the aforementioned okra and white gravy, and you could add tripe to make it a threesome). I wake up each morning with a ravenous appetite. Breakfast lasts me about two hours and then I crave munchies. I decide to eat when I am bored, when I am not bored, when I am tired, when I am rested and all the times in between.

Of course one should never refuse carefully prepared delicacies when visiting lest the hostess be insulted. At parties I feel obliged to try a little of everything, in case someone should approach later and inquire "Did you try my chocolate yo-yo cream blintzes?" Their feelings might be hurt, if, as a guest, I failed to respond positively.

Now, here I am, older and less able to digest all the wonderful things I have learned to love. Fortunately for me, you have stepped in and curbed my eating. This gentle nudge is a lot easier on me than clogged arteries.

Thank you, God.

The Rest Stop

I saw a sad little boy sitting at a table all alone at a rest stop. The family was at another table. He was ignored as they finished their meal and cleaned the table to resume their journey. I wondered why he was set aside. Did he do something wrong? He was so pitiful and sad. Did he have anything to eat? I should have made a friendly gesture toward the family and found out. He could have been an abused child.

A year or so later I was at a bus stop. A young mother with a baby and a small boy were waiting for the arrival of a bus. The mother doted and cooed at the baby but she was unreasonably harsh with the boy to the point of being vicious and hateful, mean-spirited and cruel. The small boy was not loud or seemingly doing anything to warrant her constant chastisement. His demeanor told me it was not an isolated incident. I wanted to put my arms around him but I didn't. I wanted to say, "I will take care of this child you obviously don't want." He, I knew, was an abused child, but I did nothing.

God, please don't let the cock crow the third time. Help me put aside my own fears if such a situation should arise again, and do what you would want me to do.

Hello God, it's me again,

I need to talk to you about my failings. I always try to do the right thing but I fail a lot. Could you help me a little more?

Failings of the Day

I know an elderly person who has needs and I haven't helped enough.

I spoke harshly to someone I love.

I forgot to call a friend who is in pain from losing a loved one.

In frustration I used language I shouldn't.

I sighed because it was time to address Christmas cards and I didn't take time to do it slowly and carefully.

The phone rang while I was asking the blessing of the food so I shortened the prayer.

I didn't ask your help in planning my day and things were a mess.

I bought another pair of shoes.

Fences

When I was growing up fences were built to keep cows and horses in the pastures. There were no fences between houses, unless, of course, there was a pasture between them. The fences were not there to separate neighbor from neighbor. There were no problems if one walked across a neighbor's property, or even if they picked a few wild flowers along the way. Times have changed. There are more and more fences built along "property lines" and more and more "this land is my land" attitudes. There seems to be, along with the growing tendency to build fences, a building of walls around people, resulting in a growing unfriendly attitude.

Please, God. Don't let me build a fence except to keep animals in place. Let me be accessible if anyone needs my help and don't let me build a wall between my neighbor and myself.

Servitude

The etiquette of servitude annoys me. I understand needing help and I understand paying for it. I understand that being a worker or servant is an honorable profession. One hires another person to do things one is unable, for any reason, to do for oneself.

The thing that bothers me is the "Yes, Ma'am, No, Ma'am, I bow to your bidding" part, the humbling of one human being to another, the demanding of humility of one over another. Humility is not a fault; to humble oneself of one's own volition is commendable. It is the demanding of the humility that gives me trouble. Certainly politeness is expected and the person paying should have work and duties accomplished according to their specifications. It is when the lowly servant thing is demanded that I become uncomfortable. You made me too independent. I believe you want me to do what I am paid for with pride and loving-kindness.

Road Maps

Reading road maps takes a little study to get the hang of it but once a few simple rules are learned it's easy. North is up, South is down, East to the Right and West to the left. By watching the sun one can figure out which direction one is driving, except in bad weather. Bad weather always complicates things. Of course roads do wind about so that must be kept in mind. The scenic routes can prove to be a challenge, but rewarding if one can avoid becoming lost, and one can only hope to avoid traffic jams, whether caused by an accident or road work.

Following a road map on some days is easier than others. Mondays can be bad because almost everyone had the weekend off and are anxious to begin the workweek, all "gung ho" and full of vinegar, which makes for a heavy foot on the gas pedal. On Fridays there is a rush to spend paychecks, Saturday is a big shopping day with lots of those invulnerable teen drivers out of school. Holidays are rough, too. All these things affect one's ability to "follow the map."

It is wise to refrain from trusting oneself in the "map reading-map following" agenda. One should remember that looking for short cuts is best left to experts, (I cite this from experience). It is best to trust instead either a computer trip ticket or a stop at a friendly welcome station situated near state lines. Of course, once you have instructions in hand it's up to you, the traveler, to follow them. Remember, wide lines on the map are wide roads and thin lines can lead you astray.

I'm glad you placed it on the hearts of the ancients to write down your maps and guides for living. They are a lot easier to read and have much fewer pitfalls. Please help me to stay on the wide roads so I won't get lost.

War

Why am I expected to agree with a war when I feel the Prince of Peace would disagree? Why do men fight and kill instead of finding peaceful ways to settle differences? Help me understand why some agree to study war. Is it because we have failed in small ways of conscience that now we must wrestle big wars of conscience? Your army is an army of love and peace. Help me to accept that some worship differently. Help me to love more, even those whose philosophy is not agreeable to me.

Trains

Trains stay pretty much on track. The rails match the grooves in the wheels making it difficult to take any other course except to follow the tracks. Of course there are switches in a few places that can change the course but the train is still on the tracks. Occasionally there is a catastrophe that takes a train off the tracks, but not often.

Some people get off the tracks of life. It makes living difficult for them and uncomfortable for others. Some cruise along on their track and never help or comfort fellow travelers who might need aid. They take the ride as though they deserve any perks the trip might offer but don't wish to share with others.

God, please help me stay on the track you have prepared for me, and let me be a blessing to others along the way.

Time Machines

Aren't watches wonderful? Right there on one's wrist, handy for checking to see if it's time for the children to come home from school, if it's time to start supper, how long before sundown or when a favorite program will be on television. Then there are big clocks in schoolrooms for children and scholars to check in anticipation of the freedom of recess, lunch or dismissal. There are timers on kitchen stoves and microwaves that can be set and relied upon to begin and end as programmed. Clocks have been put in cars, making it easy to plan when to eat on a long trip, as eating too soon might cause indigestion and too late lead to nervousness and exhaustion. There are clocks on town halls, in town squares, on banks and radio stations. You will find clocks for sale in stores: sunburst, grandfather, cuckoo, digital and analog. There are watches to buy; practical, ornamental, water proof for divers, diamond studded for the elite.

I think with so much help there is no excuse for being late for church or making time for daily prayer. Help me watch the clocks in life and to remember it's how I use my time that counts.

Please Give Me Patience

When someone laughs and comments, "She doesn't even know—(so on and so forth), please help me keep my big mouth shut. It seems quite ridiculous that when I ask a legitimate question from finding myself in unfamiliar surroundings, that someone must laugh at my ignorance. Using the word "even" presents the insinuation that I know nothing at all. Please close my mouth and don't let me ask them what kind of houses the Passamaquoddies built or if they know what yellow root is used for or what kind of soil is best for growing blueberries. Please help me be kind and gracious and self-effacing and have compassion for their insecurities.

Hello God,

Sometimes I behave selfishly. I'm selfish about a lot of things. For instance, there's time. I often become so absorbed in projects I enjoy that I don't want to leave them. I forget that perhaps I could give up my absorption in my own delights and help someone else, or just be company to someone who is lonely. I fail to be generous with my time.

And things. My things. You have given me a lot of things and sometimes I have trouble parting with them. I should remember that they are just on loan to me. In my heart I know they are only worldly goods but I cling to my things and have trouble giving them up. Help me share more. Remind me that it's only stuff.

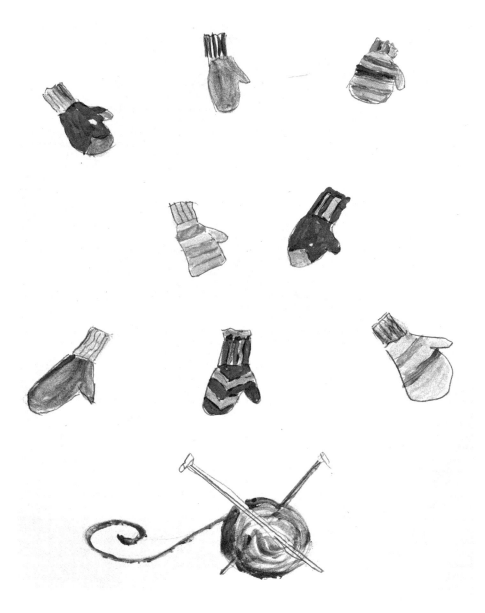

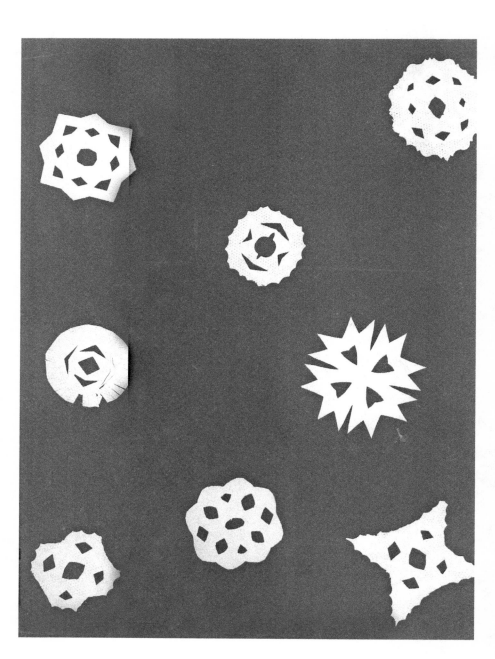

Mittens

I decided to knit mittens. It's been a rough week. I don't seem to be real good at reading and following instructions, (I guess you already knew that). They really look pretty laid out on the back of the couch. I used acrylic yarn so they are all washable, and the colors are so bright and cheery. I had hoped to give them in pairs as gifts, imagining how they would keep little fingers warm while playing in the snow, but I've been re-thinking their use. Perhaps they would make neat containers for small gifts. They could hang from the Christmas tree, filled with sugarplums and nuts and candy canes. You see, God, they are a lot like your snowflakes. Pretty, but no two alike.

Disappointment

Hello God,

Here I am, disappointed again. I'm disappointed with the day's events. I thought it was going to be a wonderful day but it wasn't. I became disappointed because someone broke a promise. I planned a small get-together but it turned out that those who had accepted the invitation went to appointments or other commitments and didn't come. I understand but I'm still disappointed. I'm also disappointed in myself. I think perhaps I should accept the situation graciously, and remember that I have failed others at times, either knowingly or unknowingly.

Please, God, help me accept my inadequacies with grace and perhaps a little laughter.

Patchwork Quilts

Quilts are amazing. Some quilt patterns are predictable, each piece arranged in symmetrical designs that are constant from one square to another, much like some folks with even temperaments. Some quilts are made of quiet pastels, serene, delicate and calm. Others fairly shout their independence, wildly vivid, their colors splashing loudly in their zeal to be noticed. Quilts can be created with a country calico look or fashioned of cotton prints and plains. They can be sewn of velvet and satin into sophisticated elegance. Some are thin and some are fat and puffy, or any thickness in between. How interesting it is to imagine the personalities of those who have sewn quilts.

I know you love your children of every color with all their different ways, and quilts seem to tell your story.

Fingers

There are also many kinds of fingers. The most obvious ones are those on our hands, also called phalanges. They are handy for sewing, painting, fruit picking, fruit peeling, weeding, planting, polishing, knitting, crocheting, marble playing, writing, aiming footballs, basketballs and baseballs. Then there is the tying of shoestrings, petting animals, weaving, quilting, and the flipping of pizza dough along with multitudes of other uses.

There are fingers of land reaching into the ocean, ladyfingers for eating at parties, fried chicken fingers for lunch at the fast food eatery, finger pointing and finger painting.

Help me to never use finger pointing in a bad way and to remember that I am not above having my faults singled out by a pointed finger.

Hello God,

There was a lot of wind this month. It rattled the windows, blew things about, howled around the eaves and blew rain against the windowpanes and sent the spring run-off rushing through the gullies. It bent trees, its powerful force violently and mercilessly swaying the defenseless branches. The limbs bent and thrashed but continually straightened once again to await the next onslaught they would be forced to endure.

Please, God, give me the strength to withstand the winds of life that might force me to bend in ways you would not approve. Let me bend when it is prudent but always return again to your ideals.

More Rocks

I have an endless fascination with rocks. They are used in so many ways. Of course we know we are to build our "house upon a rock" for stability, rather than on wash-away sand. Then there are the beautiful rock walls that delineate land boundaries, originally used to keep cattle in their own pastures. No need for branding with them soundly fenced in their own space.

Rock gardens can be planned with all kinds of flowering and non-flowering plants; climbers, crawlers, multipliers, all hugging rocks in an artful array of color against the earth tones of diversely colored stones.

Rocks of all shapes and sizes lend themselves to all kinds of uses; house foundations, whole houses, countertops, lamp bases, steps, posts and markers. We grow up walking gravel paths and strolling beaches of stones ground by the ages into a wonderful softness underfoot.

Man has been fashioning jewelry from rocks since the beginning of time, using opals, turquoise, jade, tourmaline, onyx, rubies, sapphires and of course, diamonds. Rocks can be ground and carved, and mark our final resting place when our souls leave this earth to be with you.

Thank you, God.

Sugar Maples

I wish I had several sugar maple trees. I remember when I was young living on my grandparent's farm making maple syrup was an important thing for my grandmother. The trees in the back yard were "tapped." Not the way it is done today. No special buckets, no metal or plastic tubes or spouts. Sap buckets were made by punching a hole near the rim on each side of a large can. A wire handle (usually an old coat hanger) was attached to the can by inserting the ends of the wire though the holes and bending the ends to hold it in place. The spout was a piece of alder branch deemed large and strong enough to hold a bucket of sap. Half the stick was left round for insertion into a hole drilled into the tree trunk, half was carefully whittled flat and the pith removed the whole length to allow the sap to flow through the round end and down the small trough and into the bucket. A small groove was cut in the round end to keep the bucket from sliding off. This all accomplished, the sap was ready to begin its slow drip and my grandmother had her huge kettle ready and waiting, with plenty of wood piled in the wood box in the kitchen and in the woodshed.

But Grammie wasn't the only one waiting. Small children on a farm were not privy to candy bars and ice cream, and the faintly flavored sap was too much of a temptation for my sister and me. We would sneak through the back yard, hidden by the laundry flapping on the clothesline, and tip the bucket to our lips and take a little drink. I never was sure how Grammie could have seen us or known what we were up to, but I can still hear her shrill voice, "The children are into the sap buckets! The children are into the sap buckets!" Of course then we had no inkling that it would take fifty gallons of sap to make a gallon of maple syrup, and today I feel remorse over our pilfering, but I do have a wish. I wish I had sugar maple trees that I could tap and let children take a sip whenever they wanted.

Bad Apples

One bad apple can spoil a whole bunch, conversely, one righteous person can make a difference in the scheme of things. Defining a righteous person can be difficult. What one person deems righteous, another does not. Too much time is wasted on this kind of judging. Some find it easier to find the faults of others than to realize their own blemishes. Perhaps it's a case of not seeing the woods for the trees. Help me spend more time correcting my own faults and less time seeking the faults of others.

I Don't Believe

I don't believe I've been put on this earth to ignore the needs of my fellow man.

I don't believe it's right to stand by and allow abuse of young children.

I don't believe I have the right to ridicule the beliefs of others, no matter how different their views might be from mine.

I don't believe frightening children brings them closer to you or helps them accept your love. They need to know you are a loving God.

I don't believe I've done enough to show others that your love is waiting for them.

I don't believe I could live without your constant love and care.

Things Change

Today I drove past a field of daisies blowing in the summer breeze. They covered a spot on a hill where just last year a house had stood bravely fighting against time. The few shingles that still clung to the roof were gray and worn and the outside walls of the house were frayed and cracked. Now the building that once housed a family is gone, for it was no longer useful and beyond repair. How like these fragile bodies in which we live. We, too, will be removed and hopefully, flowers will grow in our place. But we will not be like the house. We have souls that will journey far, and perhaps there will be fields of flowers there, also.

Economics

Refrigerators used to last twenty years or more. The old gas powered ones went on cooling almost forever. In modern times, with all the new technology, we find refridgerators have a five-year guarantee on the compressor while other parts are under questionable warranty. One does well to have a food cooler that will last seven years without major repairs. Of course, insurance can be purchased, although the premiums are so expensive the buyer will be paying for the appliance twice in three or four years. Lord, help me understand modern day economics.

Stairs

Falling down stairs is a jolting experience. It's so sudden there seems to be no stopping the flight until the body reaches a landing. Sometimes one can grab a railing, which contributes to the pain as the shoulder takes a jerk in the effort of trying to arrest the descent of the body weight. The pain from the fall can last weeks or even months. It's just a hint of how one can suffer when falling from your grace.

Poetry

Rhyming poetry is a lot like dancing. The wording may not be exact but the meter is all important. Many dancers perform intricate steps and even partners may move together smoothly, but if they become out of sync with the music their talent diminishes in the eyes of the beholder.

In ballroom dancing the fluid three-quarter timing results in a waltz. Good dancers glide and turn in graceful rhythm, the foxtrot promotes more pronounced movement to capture the beat. The similarity with rhyming poetry is in the selection and arrangement of the words. True poetic artistry uses words and meter together to enthrall the reader with the lyrical sound and emotion of the subject they wish to present. Reading romantic poetry should be as smooth as a waltz, but adventurous and comedic poetry as quick and exciting as a foxtrot. Lord, thank you for the many ways you have given us to express ourselves.

Boxes

My friend has a small grocery store in a modest little village. While larger stores in larger towns flatten boxes as goods are placed on shelves (for recycling purposes) my friend prefers to allow them the opportunity to be used twice before their journey to the recycling center. One finds them neatly stacked off to the right of the store entrance where any person needing a cardboard box may freely choose from the many sizes and shapes of containers there.

The variety of shapes and designs are quite interesting. Some have lids while others do not. Some are of heavy grade stock while some are flimsy, some solid, some with holes. One must be careful to choose a fitting container for a chosen project.

They are like humans of different sizes and shapes and abilities. I guess it doesn't matter, because although we may be choosy about boxes, you love us all no matter what shape we might be. Perhaps we should remember that it's not the box itself that counts, but the contents.

Molasses vs Maple Syrup

Molasses cookies are a great favorite in New England. The far northern Yankees like molasses in their baked beans, molasses in their steamed brown bread and puddings. Children enjoy "molasses and bread," (crumbled bread with ample molasses poured over it) as an afternoon snack. This southern ingredient is a great favorite in a multitude of New England recipes, although there is no sugar cane grown there and no cane presses to extract the sweet syrup from the rough sugar cane if it were. It is less popular where it is grown than where it cannot be grown. But, Oh, they love maple syrup down South. They love it on pancakes and buckwheat cakes and relish maple sugar candy. Now, with such a pleasant exchange of sweetness, why was there a war?

The Tides

The tides are endless. They work shoreward for hours. Waves, sometimes big, sometimes small (depending on the weather and the moon), fight their way to the shore with a hunger to kiss the beach; splashing joyously against rocky coasts and calmly creeping up sandy shores only to once again withdraw back to the depths of the sea. A few moments rest and then they resume the cycle of inward rushing, followed by their retreat to the wide ocean beyond. The ocean speaks of your love and care, as constant as the endless tides.

Hello God,

Here I am again, a little disheartened over my weaknesses. As I've said before, I realize I have a lot of failings. I don't mean physical weakness, or failings due to growing older. I mean weakness with little things, like putting off chores that should be done today instead of "sometime," neglecting to make time to visit a shut-in or make a phone call to someone who has suffered the loss of someone dear. Please help me plan my days better and give me a nudge to do the little things that might mean a lot to someone in need.

Children are so brave. Sometimes it's hard for me to understand why some little ones must suffer such terrible illnesses. Their stoicism is beyond understanding. When adults are crying and malingering with their suffering, the children bravely face difficult treatment with calm acceptance. Perhaps it is because they are closer to you and have had less time to wander from your care and guidance. Thank you for your aid to the innocent and help me remember to come to you as a child.

Small Feet

When I was growing up it seemed that small feet was a good thing and I worried as I matured that mine were growing much too fast. Perhaps reading about the ancient Japanese custom of binding the feet of growing children to keep their feet small influenced my thinking. I didn't realize the foot-bindings were deforming, or that it might be painful, both while growing and then walking on the deformity once it was accomplished. I was fortunate to have a wise friend who informed me that larger feet seldom hurt as they make a more solid platform to support the body. Thank you for my friend and please help me to remember that it is the size of the heart that counts, and that small is not always good.

Laundry

A day at the laundromat is very good for the soul. Watching the clothes spin is not all that exciting, but the experience gives one a little time to sort out one's thoughts, beyond the reason for being there, that is. In my case it's whenever my ever-unfaithful washing machine goes on the fritz and parts "must be ordered." The spin cycle looks really quite frantic and it gave me the opportunity to say, "Hey, wait a minute. Such violent action must be hard on my clothes." Thinking about the mad dash to the laundromat and making a mental list of all the things I needed to accomplish right away and all the things that wouldn't be accomplished because I was "wasting" time at the laundromat gave me pause. Life shouldn't be a mad, frantic whirl, and watching the spinning laundry gave me a new perspective on the constant whirl in which we live. I think slowing down might save a lot of the wear and tear of living, and I think I will be really glad when my home washing machine is repaired again. Perhaps I will set it on the gentle cycle.

Hello God, it's me again,

I have noticed that there are many hints that one is ageing. The first few strands of silver are the most easily recognized, unless one has made frequent trips to the dye-works parlor. Next, a few small lines about the eyes, easily dismissed as laugh lines or easily attributed to sun and wind exposure. Then the dentist begins giving extra warnings about gingivitis, and one realizes the expression "long of tooth" really means the "receding of gums." For men there is often the receding of the hairline, otherwise known as the lengthening of the forehead. Strangely, the hair lost on the top of the head seems to appear in the ears and nostrils. Equally shared by both sexes is the arrival of foot pain. The hated bunions on the ball of the foot appear, (just above the great toe), first discovered by several manifestations of pain. First the shoes become a little tight. This can be remedied by buying new shoes, (hurrah), but in a slightly larger size, (who could notice?). The second pain comes when one is stocking footed or bare footed and the foot is accidentally clonked against the table leg. It's difficult to control the screaming as the impact sends a message to every nerve in the body followed by groaning and clutching the painful foot in agony. The good news is that with time (a lot of it) the swelling will subside somewhat but a bony knob will remain. The larger shoes will remain. Some pain will remain. Males seem to accept the larger shoes with no angst: a slightly wider dress shoe or sneaker doesn't prove to be a problem. For the female, however, the story is different. Those sexy high heels are out, out, out! Somehow the low-heeled shoes just don't make the grade with dress-up clothes. She must now join the not so sexy, sensible group. Now more than the foot thing comes into play. Wearing the blouse outside the skirt rather than tucked in goes along with the look and dressing becomes a chore; "the right accessories over the boxy blouse above a longer skirt above sensible shoes." The right accessories must be chosen to keep the focus away from the boxy jacket over the boxy blouse above the longer skirt above the sensible shoes. Clothing is the cause of the real mid-life crisis, but it is bearable if enough attention is paid to careful dressing. Time goes by and then, as every woman knows, she has really aged when she is called "cute." Life goes from "cute" when we are born, to "neat," to "cool," to "sexy." (For males: "all boy," to "hunk," to "dignified," to "distinguished") and finally, once again, she is "cute". Please, Lord, help me through the "cute" years.

Hello God,

You've given me a lot of happiness over the years. Don't let me forget from whence all good things come.

When I leave this earth and come home to you all the alders will not have been cut, the rocks will not be moved, the trees will not be pruned, the flowers will not all be planted, and the lawn will be in need of mowing. The windows will still be waiting to be washed, the laundry will be undone and there will be dust on the mantle. I think you want me to stop worrying about it.

Jean